Introduction

With its distinctive black and white striped face and short, squat body, the badger *Meles meles* is probably one of the most popular and easily recognisable mammals in Britain. The badger is a member of the Mustelid family, along with weasels, otters and pine marten. The most recent estimate suggests that there are about 250,000 badgers in Britain, of which 25,000 are in Scotland. Yet most people have probably only glimpsed this shy creature in the car headlights at night, or have seen corpses by the side of the road as a result of a collision with a car.

Habitat

Badgers rely on a variety of habitat types for food and shelter. Although 80 per cent of setts - their underground homes - are found in woodland, badgers can be found in any area with sufficient cover of shrubs, bushes or undergrowth, a well-drained and easily dug soil, a supply of bedding material, a low level of disturbance and suitable areas for foraging within an accessible distance. 'Typical' badger habitat is a patchwork of pasture and woodland providing good areas for earthworms and foraging, as well as good areas for setts. Setts have, however, been found in unusual areas such as railway and road embankments, open fields and under buildings.

Badger setts in the Borders

Entrance to badger sett, Perthshire

Badgers are found throughout Britain, but their distribution is uneven and one third of the British population lives in the south-west of England. They are absent from parts of northern Scotland where the acidic soils provide them with little food or suitable shelter and, while small numbers can be found in some upland peaty areas, they are rarely found above 500 m. Although absent from many urban areas, badgers may be found in considerable densities in others. They are most commonly found on land below 100 m and are rarely found on intensively used arable land. In contrast, land farmed for livestock provides optimum habitat for badgers. Setts may also have been lost from apparently suitable areas as a result of historic persecution from which the local population has never recovered.

Badger emerging from woodland sett

Searching tree roots for food

Appearance

The badger is well adapted for its burrowing lifestyle, with powerful limbs and long claws on the front feet to aid with digging and foraging.

Guard hairs caught in fence

The body of the badger is covered by long guard hairs (approximately 100 mm long) which are black at the tip and root, and white in the centre which makes the coat look grey. Under these long guard hairs is a coat of short, light-coloured underfur. The hairs on the head are short and white, except for those forming the black stripes running from the base of the ears almost to the snout.

Badger footprint

Badgers moult once a year, losing their underfur first, followed by their guard hairs. New guard hairs grow first in the late summer, followed by new underfur which is most dense in the winter months. The skin is very tough but loose, which helps as a defence, making it difficult for an attacker to grip the badger's body.

Although there are no differences in the markings between male and female badgers, one slight difference between the sexes is in the shape of head. The male (boar) is more heavily built than the female, and has a shorter head, thicker neck and blunter snout. The adult female (sow) is sleeker in comparison, with a narrower head and neck. The sow's head is also flatter, and narrower between the ears. However, in practice, differences between the sexes are difficult to observe in the field and even experts can make mistakes!

Male badgers are heavier than the females with average weights of 11 kg and 10 kg respectively. However, body weight varies through the year, as animals put on fat reserves to help them survive winter months, and lose it again as they use it up over winter. The weight gain and loss depends on a number of factors, including the availability of food and whether the animal can feed daily over the winter. However, in late autumn badgers in Scotland can weigh up to one and a half times their summer weight due to extra fat which helps them to deal with the ravages of a hard, Scottish winter.

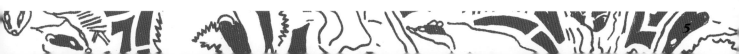

Social organisation

Badgers are sociable animals and generally live in groups of around six individuals, although groups may vary in size between two and 23 animals. They have a territory which they defend jointly, and vigorously exclude other badgers. The size of the territory is determined by the feeding habitat and not by the number of animals in the group. In good habitat, badgers may defend an average of 50 hectares (125 acres). Territories of 300 hectares (or more) have been recorded where food is scarce and badgers have had to roam wider in search of food. In contrast, this can be as little as 14 hectares in areas which are exceptionally rich in food. Badgers are often loyal to areas for many years and territories may become traditional. For example, a territory boundary which initially followed the line of a hedge may persist long after the hedge itself has been removed.

Some of the territory may not be used by the whole group, and even the dominant boar may restrict his use to certain areas at times (the 'core' range). Territorial behaviour varies seasonally, and is most apparent in spring when mating activity is at a peak. Badgers mark the edge of their territories using 'dung pits', which are grouped together as 'latrines'. The largest latrines may be found near the main sett and along territory boundaries, with less significant ones at path intersections and feeding areas. Urine forms as important a marker as faeces at these pits. Young badgers do not use latrines but urinate randomly in the home range.

Badger latrine

Badgers usually live in groups

Badgers inside sett

Breeding

Badgers become sexually mature at 12 to 15 months, although this can vary from 9 months in some sows to two years in some boars. They can mate at any time of the year. Around 80 per cent of mature females are fertilised in February/March, immediately after the birth of their young, but individuals continue to mate through the year, to another peak in August/September, when some yearling females also come into oestrus (heat) and breed for the first time.

Badgers are one of the few mammals which can suspend the development of their young in the womb by delaying implantation of the fertilised egg into the uterus wall. They are able to maintain a small ball of cells (a blastocyst) in suspended development for up to 9 months, until it implants in the womb (in December) and progresses to a pregnancy of about 7 weeks. Consequently, all the young are born between mid-January and mid-March, after which they can emerge from the sett to the warmth of spring.

Female badgers often mate with more than one male during the year. They continue to ovulate even if they have been fertilised earlier, and they are able to carry more than one blastocyst. As a result, one litter of badger cubs may be sired by different boars. Generally only one sow in the group actually produces viable cubs, as subordinate females often fail to conceive, and dominant sows may kill the offspring of any other female in the group. However, some groups may produce more than one litter. Approximately 35 per cent of social groups fail to reproduce in any year.

Cubs are born in an underground chamber lined with bedding. The number of cubs per litter ranges from one to five, with an average of two or three. Length at birth size is relatively constant (around 120 mm) although individual weights can vary between 75 g and 132 g. depending on the size of the litter. larger litters tend to contain smaller cubs. Cubs are able to forage for themselves at around 12 weeks old, but are still dependent on their mother during the summer.

Feeding

Foraging for food

Badgers are omnivorous, taking a variety of food from insects, small mammals and birds to plant foods such as fruit, nuts and crops. Earthworms form up to 50 per cent of their diet in Britain. These are particularly important in spring, when females suckling cubs require most energy, and in autumn for fattening up for the winter, but they are eaten whenever they are available. Scrapes and snout marks are the most obvious clues that badgers have been foraging in an area.

Larger animal prey may be taken when available, but the slow, rolling gait of the badger is more adapted to foraging than to active hunting. When a badger is frightened, it is capable of moving considerably faster - galloping at speeds up to 25 miles per hour - but it is not able to sustain this speed for any great distance. Badgers are not noted for their climbing skills, but individuals have also been known to scale tree trunks in search of slugs. Also, although not natural swimmers, they can do so if the need arises.

Badgers are active throughout the year although they are less active during the winter months. They are primarily a nocturnal animal but it is not impossible to see them out during daylight hours. They generally emerge from their setts around dusk to forage during the summer months, but may not appear until after dark during winter. Badgers do not hibernate but are able to conserve their energy by reducing their body temperature by a few degrees. They can also go without food for more than a week by relying on their fat reserves put on in the autumn.

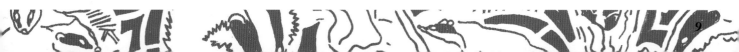

The sett

The sett is the underground structure in which the badger social group lives and shelters through the day. There are four types of sett.

Main sett :   there is usually only one main sett per social group. This is used continuously and may have well-used paths leading to it. It will have a number of entrances, either used or disused, and many have active spoil heaps outside the entrance. Occasionally, where conditions are relatively poor, badgers may have a large territory with a scatter of smaller setts

Annexe sett :   usually around 150 m from the main sett (although often closer), the annexe sett will also have well used entrances and paths connecting it to the main sett, but may not be in use all of the time.

Subsidiary sett :   these are not obviously connected to a main sett and may be some distance away. Although they may have up to five or six holes, they are, again, not always in use.

Outlying sett :   these have only one or two holes with no obvious paths connecting them to other setts. The small spoil heaps at the entrance may be small and often the holes are rarely used.

Badgers and people

Many badger setts are found on managed land. It is therefore inevitable that they come into contact with human activities although the extent to which this happens depends on a number of factors, for example the number of badgers in the area. Badgers often live close to human habitation without any disturbance at all. However, this is not always the case and interactions between people and badgers can cause problems for both.

Foraging

The most common cause of damage by badgers occurs as a result of their foraging habits, as they dig up land in search of food. This type of damage can be quite severe and is most noticeable on flat, cultivated or managed areas such as golf courses, gardens or agricultural land. Although crops may be eaten, they may also be rolled on or flattened as an incidental result of the foraging process. However, the amount of damage which this causes is not usually very significant.

Measures may be taken to keep badgers out of affected areas by appropriate fencing. Where this does not work, further actions may be considered to address the problem. Advice on how to prevent damage to crops and property should be sought from the Scottish Office Agriculture, Environment and Fisheries Department (see Badgers and the Law).

A sett entrance in an arable field

Typical signs of a badger feeding area

Digging

Badger digging out sett

Digging or burrowing to construct tunnels and setts may also create problems locally. These usually arise as tunnels undermine buildings, walls or roads, making them unsafe. This can also cause problems for heavy machinery, such as tractors, where badgers dig tunnels beneath the ground in fields or woodland. Where this happens, advice should be sought from local SOAEFD or SNH offices as to how to proceed.

This problem may also arise in relation to ancient monuments, where badgers damage historic sites. Provision is made in the Protection of Badgers Act 1992 enabling SNH to issue licences to interfere with a sett in order to preserve or investigate ancient monuments scheduled under Section 1 of the Ancient Monuments and Archaeological Areas Act 1979.

Forestry

Badger setts are most common in woodland areas. This means that they are particularly susceptible to damage or disturbance from forestry operations such as timber felling, extraction or mechanical cultivation. Badger setts are protected by law (see Badgers and the Law) and it is therefore important to ensure that action is taken to safeguard them.

Guidelines have been published by the Forestry Commission, in conjunction with the statutory nature conservation agencies and government Departments, giving advice on the law concerning badger setts, practices which will minimise disturbance and/or damage, and where and how to obtain further advice. The contact address for this information can be found at the back of this booklet.

Badger baiting

Badger digging (extracting badgers from their setts using spades and terriers) and baiting (organising, as a spectator sport, a fight between a badger and one or more dogs) have been practised in Britain since the early 1900s when badgers were considered vermin and were hunted ruthlessly. Although not known to be a widespread activity in Scotland, badger digging still occurs today in some areas and may be responsible for their extinction locally. Badgers may also be removed from Scotland, by digging, for baiting elsewhere in Britain. Initial legislation was introduced in 1973 outlawing these practices, making it illegal to kill, injure or take a badger. Efforts by the law enforcing authorities continue today to eliminate this merciless activity. Anyone becoming aware of any evidence suggesting that badger digging or baiting is going on in an area should inform the Police immediately. You should NOT approach anyone at the site.

Badgers and bovine TB

Badgers are known to carry the bacterium which causes TB in cattle. Existing evidence suggests that they may be a reservoir for the disease in the wild, possibly contributing to the continuation of bovine TB in dairy herds. The problem of bovine TB is most intense in south west England and has been recorded only once in cattle in Scotland during recent years. Research continues to try and identify the precise link between badgers and cattle, to provide an appropriate test for the disease in live animals, and to establish an effective policy for the control of infected badgers.

Road traffic accidents

Road accidents continue to be the largest cause of death in badgers. Measures, such as underpasses and fencing, are currently available to help avoid this problem, although new measures continue to be developed. The suitability and feasibility of these obviously needs to be considered at each site. Further details of these methods should be sought through local SNH or SOAEFD offices.

Helping badgers

Development of land

Development can have significant impacts on badgers, their sett and foraging resource. Developers and planners should consult SNH at the earliest possible stage.

Badgers are very sensitive to noise and movement and watching them can, be very difficult. Although it is legal to observe them quietly from a distance, they (and their setts) are protected by law from deliberate interference and care must be taken to ensure that they are not disturbed. Their nocturnal habits also make them difficult to watch. If you are lucky enough to have a badger sett nearby, it may be possible to see the cubs out playing at dusk in the summer months. For many people the most they see of badgers are the distinctive scrapes and snout marks left by their hunt for food.

Several local groups have been established to enable volunteers to help in badger conservation in their areas. Contacts for these groups may be obtained from SNH or the National Federation of Badger Groups (address on back page).

Cubs foraging for food on a rotten tree

Badgers and the law

This section is a guide to the law. For further details, please refer to the complete copies of the relevant Acts.

Badgers are protected in Britain by the Protection of Badgers Act 1992. The following provides a brief summary of the provisions of this legislation, under which it is an offence to:

- wilfully kill, injure, take, possess or cruelly ill-treat a badger, or attempt to do so;
- to interfere with a sett by damaging or destroying it;
- obstruct access to, or any entrance of, a badger sett
- disturb a badger when it is occupying a sett.

Where these are unavoidable, there is provision for some activities to be carried out under licence. Scottish Natural Heritage and the Scottish Office Agriculture, Environment and Fisheries Department (SOAEFD) share the responsibility of licensing (see below)

Badgers are also protected under the Wild Mammals (Protection) Act 1996 which makes it illegal to subject badgers to any wilful act of cruelty or abuse.

Activities which may be licensed under the Protection of Badgers Act 1992

Responsibility of Scottish Natural Heritage:

- Kill, take or interfere with a sett for scientific, conservation or educational purposes;
- Take, sell or have in possession badgers for zoological gardens or collections;
- Take for marking or ringing;
- Interfere with a sett for development under the Town and Country Planning (Scotland) Act 1972;
- Interfere with a sett for preservation or investigation of archaeological monuments;
- Interfere with a sett to investigate an offence;
- Interfere with a sett for the purpose of fox control to protect livestock, game or wildlife.

Responsibility of SOAEFD:

- Kill or take badgers, or interfere with a sett to prevent the spread of disease
- Kill or take badgers, or interfere with a sett to prevent serious damage to land, crops, poultry and property;
- Interfere with a sett for agricultural or forestry operations;
- Interfere with a sett for the purpose of land drainage.
- Interfere with a sett for the purpose of fox control to protect livestock, game or wildlife.